EDGE BOOKS

THRILLING SPORTS CARS

by Karen Latchana Kenney

Consultant:
Lisa Noble
President and CEO
Sports Car Club of America
Topeka, Kansas

CAPSTONE PRESS
a capstone imprint

Edge Books are published by Capstone Press,
1710 Roe Crest Drive, North Mankato, Minnesota 56003
www.capstonepub.com

Library of Congress Cataloging-in-Publication Data
Kenney, Karen Latchana, author.
Thrilling sports cars / by Karen Latchana Kenney.
pages cm.—(Edge books. Dream cars)
Summary: "Discusses sports cars, including their history, popular models past
and present, and how sports car owners can enjoy their cars in shows and
races"—Provided by publisher.
Audience: Ages 8-14.
Audience: Grades 4 to 6.
Includes bibliographical references and index.
ISBN 978-1-4914-2013-3 (library binding)
ISBN 978-1-4914-2184-0 (eBook pdf)
1. Sports cars—Juvenile literature. I. Title.
TL236.K46 2015
629.222'1—dc23   2014021763

Editorial Credits
Carrie Braulick Sheely, editor; Heidi Thompson, designer; Pamela J. Mitsakos,
media researcher; Katy LaVigne, production specialist

Photo Credits
Alamy: © Dan Lamont, 27,© Pat McNulty, 12, PhotoKratky – Editorial, 24, 25,
© WENN, 28; CORBIS:© Bettmann, 9, 10, © Martyn Goddard, 18–19; Dreamstime:
© Hanhanpeggy, cover,© Eric Sison, 6–7; Newscom: picture alliance/J.W. Alker,
15, picture-alliance/dpa/Uli Deck, 5, Abaca/Loona, 29, SWNS / Splash News, 16,
ZUMAPRESS/Top Gear, 20, ZUMA Press/Jasen Vinlove, 23

Design Element: Shutterstock: iconizer, welcomia, (throughout)

Printed in the United States of America in Stevens Point, Wisconsin
102014   008479WZS15

Table of Contents

STYLE AND SPEED

The 2015 California T by Ferrari is far from an ordinary car. It's ultra-sleek, and its mega power makes it incredibly fast. The Ferrari name is well known. This Italian carmaker has made popular sports cars since the 1950s.

Ferrari's new and improved California T model was big news when it came out in 2014. Its engine has twin *turbochargers*. The California T was the first turbocharged car Ferrari had made in years. The car can go from 0 to 62 miles (100 kilometers) per hour in just 3.6 seconds. It reaches a top speed of 196 miles (315 km) per hour.

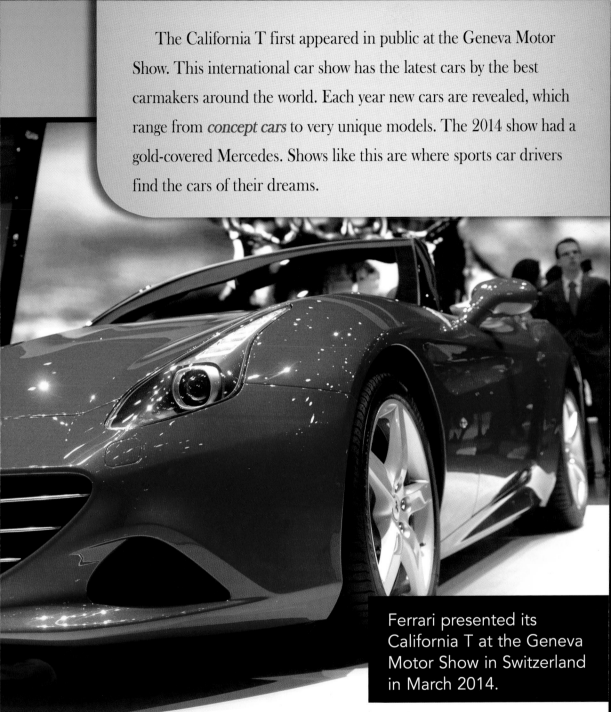

The California T first appeared in public at the Geneva Motor Show. This international car show has the latest cars by the best carmakers around the world. Each year new cars are revealed, which range from *concept cars* to very unique models. The 2014 show had a gold-covered Mercedes. Shows like this are where sports car drivers find the cars of their dreams.

Ferrari presented its California T at the Geneva Motor Show in Switzerland in March 2014.

turbocharger—a fan-driven system that connects to a car's exhaust and pushes air and fuel into the engine's cylinders; a turbocharger increases the engine's power

concept car—a car built to test an idea that is not yet available for people to buy

Cars with Attitude

That speed and sleek look—it's what makes a sports car stand out from other cars. Sports cars have a certain attitude—one that attracts car enthusiasts all over the world.

Sports cars have several features in common. Most sports cars are small with two doors. They have more *horsepower* than regular passenger cars. They are also lightweight. These features mean that sports cars can reach very high speeds. Looks also are important in sports cars. Every feature is carefully crafted, from the car's wheels to its body shape and rear *spoiler*.

Yet sports cars are more than just *street-legal* cars that can go fast. They also make great racing machines. Many sports car owners take their cars to racetracks to compete.

horsepower–a unit for measuring an engine's power
spoiler–a wing-shaped part attached to the front or rear of a sports car that improves the car's handling and keeps air from lifting the car off the road
street legal–able to be driven on public roads legally

Some sports cars have only one seat. The Lamborghini Egoista has a cockpit modeled after the cockpit of a fighter jet.

A driver puts a Lamborghini's speed to the test on a racetrack.

A FAST HISTORY

The cars of the late 1800s to early 1900s were experiments. They were made to replace carriages pulled by horses. Some early cars used steam for power. Because they lacked safety features, many were dangerous. But the cars took people where they wanted to go.

Many early cars looked very basic, including Ford's popular Model T. It came only in black. The car had a simple engine and reached a top speed of about 40 miles (64 km) per hour. Its controls looked more like ones made for a tractor or lawn mower than a car. But it was fairly simple to drive for the average person, and it was affordable.

 **Fact**

Regular cars in the early 1900s could reach top speeds of about 25 to 50 miles (40 to 80 km) per hour.

The fastest early cars were the ones built for racing on long, curved stretches of road. Some of the first races were held in the late 1800s. In 1911 cars roared down the track at the first Indianapolis 500. In the end American driver Ray Harroun claimed victory in his Marmon Wasp. Many of the fastest cars were from Europe. The Darracq from France set records. In 1905 it reached a top speed of 120 miles (193 km) per hour.

Ray Harroun drives his Marmon Wasp at the 1911 Indianapolis 500 in Indiana.

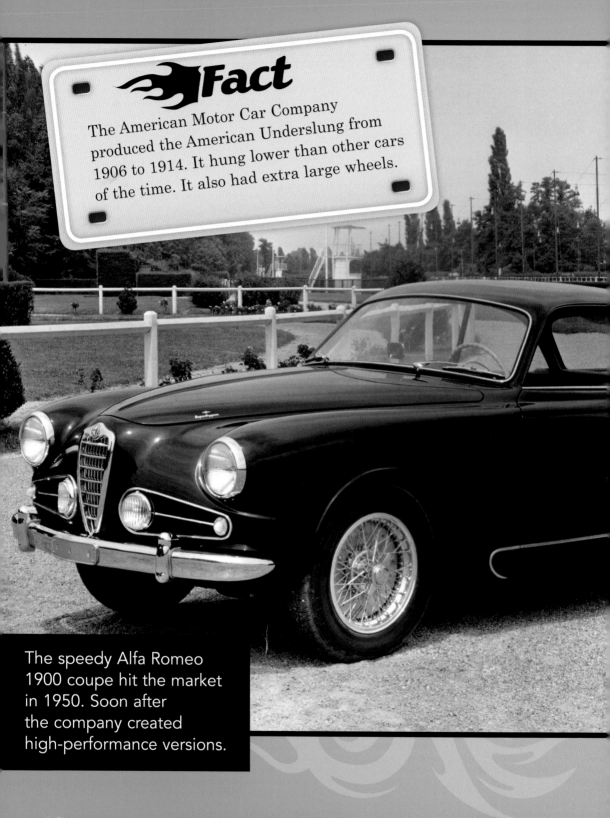

The speedy Alfa Romeo 1900 coupe hit the market in 1950. Soon after the company created high-performance versions.

From Race Cars to Road Cars

Sports car production really took off in the 1920s. Fast cars were no longer just for the racetracks. Drivers, especially wealthy ones, wanted fast cars for the roads as well. Carmakers developed ways to make cars faster. Many early cars had front-wheel drive. Making sports cars with rear-wheel drive improved the cars' *traction*. Some carmakers focused on making the engines and mechanical parts better. Other carmakers focused on making cars lighter and sleeker. All of these changes had the same purpose—speed.

Several early sports cars stood out among the crowd. In Italy the Alfa Romeo 6C 1750 became a sports car star of the early 1930s. Its lightweight body was made with aluminum. Bugatti introduced its Type 43 in 1927. Its engine had a *supercharger*. The growling engine pushed the car as fast as 110 miles (177 km) per hour.

traction—the grip of a car's tires on the ground
supercharger—a belt-driven system that connects to a car's engine and pushes air and
fuel into the engine's cylinders; a supercharger increases the engine's power

Early Speedsters

Car	Year Built	Top Speed
Mercedes-Benz Type S 36/220	1926	106 mph (171 kph)
Alfa Romeo P2	1924	123 mph (198 kph)
Bugatti Type 35B	1927	127 mph (204 kph)
Delage V-12	1923	143 mph (230 kph)
Fiat Mephistopheles	1923	146 mph (235 kph)

The first Corvettes were available only as convertibles.

Fact

The DeLorean sports car from the 1980s looked futuristic. It had *gull-wing doors* and a stainless steel body. The car was featured in the blockbuster movie *Back to the Future*.

Sports Cars Grow Up

Sports cars took a back seat to more practical cars during World War II (1939–1945). But faster, sleeker cars came back in style during the 1950s. The demand forced carmakers to improve sports car design. They put car bodies lower to the ground. This made the cars more *aerodynamic*. Looks became more important too. With features such as rounded bodies and standout colors, sports cars were even more appealing to fans.

Jaguar, Porsche, Mercedes-Benz, and Lotus became some of the big European sports carmakers. Chevrolet made its now-famous Corvette in 1953. It had a lightweight body and its V-8 engine packed a lot of power. The Porsche 911 rolled onto the market in 1963. It has been a best seller ever since.

Since the 1960s new sports cars have helped to improve car design further. In the 1970s car bodies had sharper, more angular lines than earlier cars. In the 1980s turbochargers came on the scene. Many 1990s sports cars had folding hardtop roofs. Since 2000 almost every carmaker has designed a sports car of its own. With so many new designs, sports cars have become faster and more efficient than ever before.

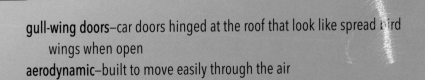

gull-wing doors—car doors hinged at the roof that look like spread bird wings when open
aerodynamic—built to move easily through the air

DESIGNED FOR PERFORMANCE

You can usually spot a sports car cruising down the road right away. Sports cars have a unique look. They are low to the ground. They have smooth, rounded bodies. They have certain *proportions* as well. The hood is usually long, while the trunk is short. Most sports car cockpits are smaller than those of passenger cars.

Sports cars come in different styles. Although many have only two seats, some also have two small rear seats. Many sports cars are coupes, which have two doors and a fully attached hardtop roof. A convertible is sometimes called a roadster. It has a top that can open. A grand tourer is a high-performance sports car that can run well for long distances. Grand tourers are larger and heavier than other sports cars.

Fact

Jaguar's designers specially built the XKR-S grand tourer's exhaust system. It delivers a unique, powerful roar.

The Aston Martin Vanquish has a V-12 engine that blasts the grand tourer to a top speed of about 183 miles (295 km) per hour.

McLaren F1 interior

Inside the Cockpit

The interiors of sports cars vary widely. Some are very basic. They are more like race cars inside. They might not have carpet on the floor. The 1990 Porsche Carrera RS was stripped down inside. The carmakers wanted to make the car as lightweight as possible. It didn't have power windows or power mirrors, and the doors had simple frames.

Other interiors are decked out with luxuries and conveniences. The McLaren F1 has a central driver's seat and two side passenger seats. The central driver's seat provides the best possible view for the driver. All controls are easy to find in the car. The interior features are lightweight, including the seats. Although the seats have very little padding, they are designed to be comfortable.

Fact

The 1958 Porsche 356's interior had a wooden steering wheel. Drivers found that the wheel could easily splinter during crashes. The sharp pieces of wood pierced drivers' hands and bodies. Drivers replaced them with metal steering wheels to make the cars safer to drive.

Acceleration

How fast does it *accelerate*? The answer is what every sports car driver wants to know. It's a big measure of a sports car's performance. A sports car's acceleration is usually measured by how fast it can go from 0 to 60 or 62 miles (97 or 100 km) per hour. In top sports cars, that can take just a few seconds.

Balance affects how well sports cars accelerate and handle high speeds. The location of the engine is one factor carmakers consider. Many sports cars have engines in the middle or rear. The mid-engine gives the best balance. The 1966 Lamborghini Miura was one of the first mid-engine sports cars. Rear engines help boost acceleration and speed in rear-wheel drive cars. The engine weight over the drive wheels helps the cars grip the road. But although this set-up helps cars with speed, it can cause problems with steering. The rear-engine Porsche 911 is a good example. It can oversteer around turns.

Super Acceleration

Sports Car	Seconds from 0 to 62 mph (100 kph)
Lamborghini Aventador	2.9
Porsche 911 Turbo S	3.1
Ferrari F12berlinetta	3.1
McLaren 12C	3.3
Aston Martin One 77	3.7
Jaguar F-Type R	4.0

Porsche put its first 911s on the market in 1964. The cars were an instant success, and modern 911s continue to be popular.

accelerate—to increase the speed of a moving object

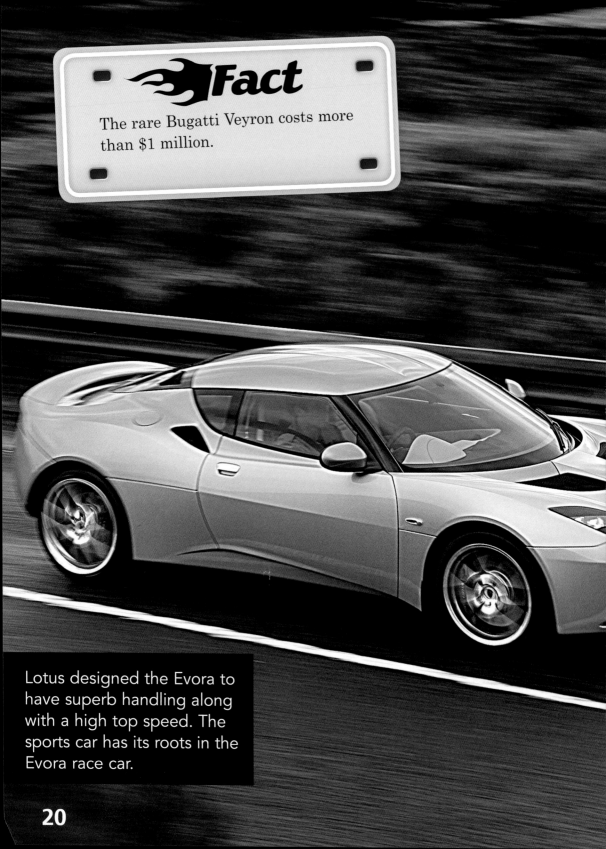

Lotus designed the Evora to have superb handling along with a high top speed. The sports car has its roots in the Evora race car.

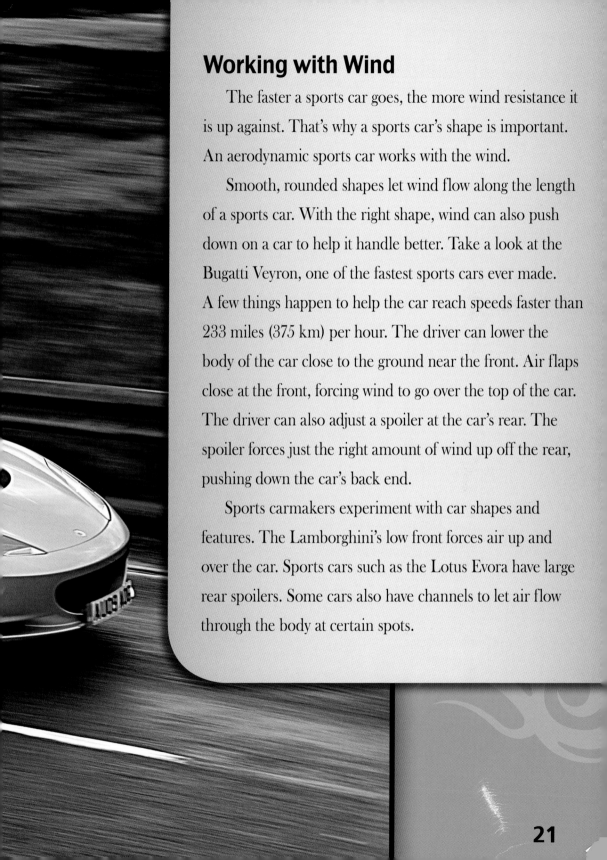

Working with Wind

The faster a sports car goes, the more wind resistance it is up against. That's why a sports car's shape is important. An aerodynamic sports car works with the wind.

Smooth, rounded shapes let wind flow along the length of a sports car. With the right shape, wind can also push down on a car to help it handle better. Take a look at the Bugatti Veyron, one of the fastest sports cars ever made. A few things happen to help the car reach speeds faster than 233 miles (375 km) per hour. The driver can lower the body of the car close to the ground near the front. Air flaps close at the front, forcing wind to go over the top of the car. The driver can also adjust a spoiler at the car's rear. The spoiler forces just the right amount of wind up off the rear, pushing down the car's back end.

Sports carmakers experiment with car shapes and features. The Lamborghini's low front forces air up and over the car. Sports cars such as the Lotus Evora have large rear spoilers. Some cars also have channels to let air flow through the body at certain spots.

THE REAL TEST

Sports cars cannot reach top speeds on regular roads. Drivers would be breaking the law if they did. Racing is the real test for sports cars.

Drivers race sports cars in professional and *amateur* sports car races. Sports car races test the limits of cars. Endurance races last for many miles and hours. A team of drivers races one car. Each driver takes a turn driving during the race. The winning car drives the longest distance during a set time. One of the longest distance records was set in 1982. At the 24 Hours of Daytona, racers drove a Porsche 935 a total of 2,666 miles (4,291 km)!

amateur—describes a sport that athletes take part in for pleasure rather than for money

Sports cars compete in the Brickyard Grand Prix at Indianapolis Motor Speedway in 2014.

Pro Racing

Many carmakers sponsor teams of pro drivers for sports car races. The cars they race fall into two main types, Grand Touring (GT) and prototype. A GT car looks like a regular sports car on the outside. But it has been specially built for racing. For example, the engines are better and the brakes are more powerful. A prototype is fully designed for racing. It looks very different from sports cars on public roads.

Drivers Allan McNish, Loïc Duval, and Tom Kristensen won the 2013 Le Mans race in their Audi R18 (#2).

One famous pro sports car race is the 24 Hours of Le Mans. This annual French race lasts for 24 hours. Part of the course is set on closed-off public roads through the town of Le Mans. It is a tough race to win. Danish driver Tom Kristensen is one of the best drivers. He is the only person to have been on the winning team of the 24 Hours of Le Mans nine times.

Current Top Sports Car Racers

Racer	Country	Wins
Allan McNish	Scotland	won a World Endurance Championship title in 2013; won three 24 Hours of Le Mans titles
Jordan Taylor	U.S.A.	won Rolex Sports Car Series Daytona Prototype Championship in 2013; second in Rolex Sports Car Series GT Championship in 2011
John Edwards	U.S.A.	won four Rolex Sports Car Series GT races in 2013
Scott Pruett	U.S.A.	won Rolex Sports Car Series Daytona Prototype Championship 2010-2012

Drivers McNish, Kristensen, and Duval (left to right) hold up their trophy after their 2013 Le Mans win.

Amateur Racing

Racing is not just for the pros. Amateur sports car owners love to test their cars on racetracks too. The Sports Car Club of America (SCCA) holds both amateur and pro races across the United States. Amateur drivers can get a special license to race after going through training. They attend racing schools, learn racing rules, and pass tests.

The U.S. Majors Tour is a series for amateur drivers that qualifies them for the SCCA National Championship Runoffs race. Top racers compete in a series of races around the United States each year. They hope that their ability in the series earns them an invitation to the Runoffs. Top drivers in the series have included Elliott Skeer and Jesse Prather.

Many other amateur races take place in certain regions of the country. The best drivers move up from these regional championships to compete in the Majors Tour.

Fact

Some celebrities race sports cars. Actors Patrick Dempsey, Paul Newman, and Steve McQueen have been some of the best celebrity racers.

A driver competes in an SCCA autocross event in Washington.

The Sports Car Club of America

The SCCA formed in 1944. Today it has more than 60,000 members in 115 U.S. regions. The club sponsors more than 2,000 races each year. Its series include the U.S. Majors Tour and the BFGoodrich Tires SCCA Super Tour. Some famous racers got their start in the SCCA, including Michael Andretti. Some recent stars of the SCCA circuit are Graham Rahal, Sam Hornish Jr., and J.R. Hildebrand.

Future Fastest Cars

Everyone wants to know what carmakers will dream up next. But new sports car concepts are tightly kept secrets. They are given secret code names. Concept cars have to be tested and tweaked. Sometimes spies snap photos of these new sports cars. Rumors then quickly spread about the latest speed machines.

Some carmakers make concept cars that challenge sports car design. Danish carmaker Koenigsegg made a car with a carbon fiber body and specially designed carbon fiber racing tires. Called the One:1, it is expected to challenge current speed records.

Sports cars gain speed and handle roads better each year. The fastest sports car world record continues to be chased by manufacturers. At the same time, millions of fans hope to catch a peek of the latest and greatest machines these companies have to offer. Their secret new designs will be the scorching sports cars of the future.

Lamborghini celebrated its 50th anniversary in 2013 by revealing the Egoista concept car.

The Koenigsegg One:1
attracts onlookers at the
Geneva Motor Show in
Switzerland in March 2014.

GLOSSARY

accelerate (ak-SEL-uh-rayt)—to increase the speed of a moving object

aerodynamic (air-oh-dye-NA-mik)—built to move easily through the air

amateur (AM-uh-chur)—describes a sport that people take part in for pleasure rather than for money

concept car (KAHN-sept KAR)—a car built to test an idea that is not yet available for people to buy

efficient (uh-FI-shuhnt)—not wasteful of time or energy

gull-wing doors (GUHL-WING DORZ)—car doors hinged at the roof that look like spread bird wings when open

horsepower (HORSS-pou-ur)—a unit for measuring an engine's power

proportion (pruh-POR-shuhn)—the relation of one part to another

prototype (PROH-tuh-type)—a type of sports car used in sports car races such as the Rolex Sports Car Series; a prototype also refers to a vehicle built to test a new design

spoiler (SPOY-lur)—a wing-shaped part attached to the front or rear of a sports car that improves the car's handling and keeps air from lifting the car off the road

street legal (STREET LEE-guhl)—able to be driven on public roads legally

supercharger (SOO-pur-char-juhr)—a belt-driven system that connects to a car's engine and pushes air and fuel into the engine's cylinders; a supercharger increases the engine's power

traction (TRAK-shuhn)—the grip of a car's tires on the ground

turbocharger (TUR-boh-char-juhr)—a fan-driven system that connects to a car's exhaust and pushes air and fuel into the engine's cylinders; a turbocharger increases the engine's power

READ MORE

Hamilton, John. *Sports Cars.* Speed Zone. Minneapolis: ABDO Pub., 2013.

Kenney, Karen Latchana. *The Science of Car Racing.* The Science of Speed. North Mankato, Minn.: Capstone Press, 2014.

Woods, Bob. *Smokin' Sports Cars.* Fast Wheels! Berkeley Heights, N.J.: Speeding Star, an imprint of Enslow Publishers, Inc., 2013.

INTERNET SITES

FactHound offers a safe, fun way to find Internet sites related to this book. All of the sites on FactHound have been researched by our staff.

Here's all you do:

Visit *www.facthound.com*

Type in this code: 9781491420133

INDEX

Enid Blyton
BIBLE STORIES

David the Shepherd Boy

ILLUSTRATED BY STEPHANIE McFETRIDGE BRITT

HARVEST HOUSE PUBLISHERS
Eugene, Oregon 97402

DAVID THE SHEPHERD BOY
Copyright © 1996 Angus Hudson Ltd.,
Great Britain/Tim Dowley & Peter Wyart
trading as Three's Company
Text copyright © 1949 and 1996 by
Darrell Waters Ltd.

Published in the United States of
America by Harvest House Publishers
Eugene, Oregon 97402

Worldwide co-edition organized and
produced by
Angus Hudson Ltd.,
London NW7 3SA
First published in 1996 by Candle Books

ISBN 1-56507-752-0

Designed and created by
Three's Company, London
Illustrated by Stephanie McFetridge Britt
The Enid Blyton Signature is a registered
Trademark ™ of Darrell Waters Ltd.,
Great Britain

Printed in Singapore
97 98 99 00 01 02/10 9 8 7 6 5 4 3 2 1

David the Shepherd Boy

The king of Israel was Saul, whom the old priest Samuel had chosen to rule over the people. For some years the king pleased Samuel, and then he quarreled bitterly with him.

Samuel went away, sorry he had chosen such a king for his people.

One day the voice of God came to Samuel.

"Go to Bethlehem, to Jesse's house. I have chosen a king from his sons."

So Samuel went to the city of Bethlehem.

"Do you come in peace?" asked the watchman.

"I come to hold a feast," said Samuel. "Go to Jesse. Tell him he is to come and bring his sons with him."

The man went and told Jesse. Jesse was a farmer, and he felt glad that such a great man as Samuel should ask for him. So he and his sons dressed in their best clothes and went to the place where the feast was to be held.

Samuel was there, waiting, for he knew God had chosen one of Jesse's sons to be king.

"Tell your sons to come before me," said Samuel. So the young men stood in front of him, strong, fully-grown, and good to look at. Samuel wondered which was to be king. He looked at each carefully.

But God spoke to him, "Not this one. Nor is this the one, nor even this one." It seemed as if not one of Jesse's sons was to be chosen after all.

Samuel was puzzled. Then he turned to Jesse. "Are all your sons here?" he asked.

"All but one, and he is only a boy," said Jesse. "He guards the sheep. He is too young to come to the feast."

"Bring him here," said Samuel. So one of the brothers went to fetch the boy. His name was David, and he was the youngest. He sat guarding the sheep, singing in the sunshine.

He was not very old, but his face was brown and healthy, and his voice was sweet when he sang. He

could make music too, and everyone loved him.

"Come quickly, David!" shouted his brother. "Come to the feast!"

The boy was full of joy, for he longed to go with his brothers. He ran after him gladly and came before Samuel, his cheeks red with running, his eyes bright.

"Now here is the boy whom God has chosen," Samuel thought. So he went to David and blessed him. When he was old enough, David would be king over all the people.

Then the feast was held, and David joined in, happy but puzzled. He did not know why Samuel had asked for him to come, but he liked the old man.

After the feast Samuel went home, and David went back to his sheep. It was not time for him to be king. He was only a boy.

But he was a boy that everyone knew and loved. Sometimes he played to his sheep, leading them from place to place, and they loved him and followed him.

David was a good shepherd. He guarded his flocks well. He had a sling and with it he could hurl a stone a long way and make it hit its mark.

When a lion and a bear came to kill his sheep, David sprang up and ran at them. He killed the lion, and then he killed the bear. He was the bravest of all the brothers though he was the youngest.

Samuel often sent for David. He taught him the laws of God, and told him to obey them, for then he would be a wise and good ruler.

Then he would send David back to his sheep, and the boy would think of all he had learned. He would make songs and sing them while his sheep nibbled the grass and listened.

Saul was still the king of Israel. But he was an unhappy man; sometimes fits of madness came over him.

Then he would call for music to be played, for that was the only thing that brought him peace. His servants feared to see him so sad and gloomy.

One day one of them spoke to him: "Won't you have someone to play upon the harp? I know a youth who would please you greatly. He is David, a son of Jesse the farmer."

Then messengers were sent to Jesse. "Our master, King Saul, commands you to send to him your son David," they said.

So David got ready to go to the king. He took his harp with him. Soon he was standing before poor, unhappy Saul.

Saul liked David at once. "You must stay with me and be my armor-bearer," he said. "You shall play and sing to me when I am troubled."

So David stayed with Saul the King, and when he played upon his harp, the king forgot his sadness and was glad.

The Giant, Goliath

David stayed with Saul for a time and then went back to his father's sheep. One day his brothers told him that their old enemies, the Philistines, had come to fight against them once more.

"Three of us are going to fight them," his brothers told him. "If we want food, we will send word, and you must bring us bread and cheeses."

David watched his brothers go. When the message came that they wanted food, he was glad. Now he would be able to see the enemy—and perhaps even watch a battle. He took food with him and went over the hills to find his brothers.

Now, as he talked with his brothers, David saw an amazing sight. In the Philistines' camp was a giant called Goliath. He was an enormous man, tall and broad and strong.

Every day he marched out of the camp dressed in a coat of mail and a great helmet of brass. In front of him marched a man carrying his great shield, and in the giant's hand was a long spear.

The giant shouted at the top of his loud voice, "Bring me a man to fight with! If he kills me, then the Philistines shall be your servants. If I kill him, you shall be ours and serve us. Where is the army of Israel? Can you not send one man to fight me?"

The Israelites were afraid of this giant. No one went to fight him. Some even ran away when he appeared. David was amazed to hear him; and to see the fear on his brothers' faces.

"Who will go to fight this giant?" asked David. But no man went.

"How dare he defy us!" cried David. "I will go to fight him myself!"

King Saul heard his words and laughed. "You are only a boy," he said, "and this man has been a soldier for years."

"I have killed a lion and a bear," said David. "God will help me against this Philistine too."

"Then go," said Saul, and gave him armor. David put on a coat of mail, and a heavy helmet, and strapped a great sword to his side.

"I cannot walk in these," said David, and took them off. He picked up his stick and went down to the brook and chose five smooth stones. He put them into his shepherd's bag. Then he took his sling and went to meet the giant Goliath.

Down the opposite hillside came the giant. He saw that David carried a staff and he laughed.

"Am I a dog to be beaten with a stick!" he roared.

Then David ran toward the giant, putting one of the smooth, round stones into his sling as he went. He flung the stone at the giant with all his might.

It hit Goliath in the middle of his forehead. The stone sank in and killed the giant. He fell down on his face, dead. David ran to him, took up his sword and cut off the giant's head. A cry of fear went up from the watching Philistines. They fled away in dismay, and Saul's men ran down the hillside to chase them.

It was a great victory for Israel. David was a hero; King Saul praised and rewarded him.

"Return no more to your sheep," he said. "Stay with me and I will make you a captain in my army."

So David stayed with Saul. His great friend was Jonathan, the king's own son. The two were closer than brothers.

David soon became a great captain, leader of all Saul's men. Saul loved him and spoke well of him. But one day Saul turned against him.

There had been another victory, and the women went out to meet David, singing songs of praise. Saul heard the words and was angry.

"Saul has slain his thousands, and David his ten thousands!" sang the women.

These words made Saul jealous.

Then Saul lost all his love for David and made up his mind to kill him. At times David had to flee from Saul. Then Jonathan would miss David very much.

After a time Saul made his peace with David, and David came back to his palace. Jonathan wept with joy to see him again. David took his harp and often played to Saul when sadness came over him.

But one day, as David was sitting playing to him, Saul suddenly took up a spear and flung it at the young man. It did not hit him but struck the wall. David ran from the room and would go to Saul no more.

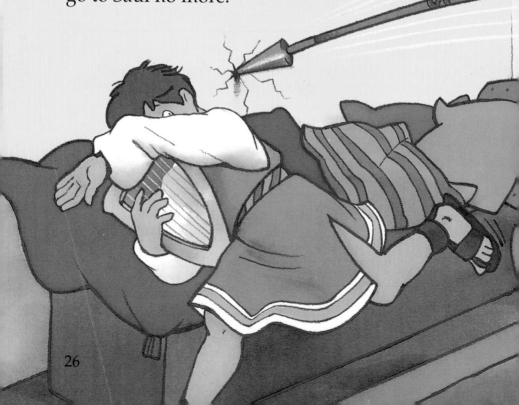

There came a great battle with the Philistines, in which Saul and his sons went to fight. Then sad news was brought to David.

"Saul the King is killed and all his sons—Jonathan with them," said the messenger. David wept for Jonathan his friend, whom he had loved so much.

"You shall be our king," said the people of Israel to David. "You shall rule over us and lead us in battle!"

And so David, who had been a shepherd boy, became king of Israel and ruled for many years.